The New Novello Choral Edition

J. H. MAUNDER

Olivet to Calvary

for tenor and baritone soli, SATB and organ

Text written and arranged by
Shapcott Wensley

Revised by Michael Pilkington

Order No: NOV 072487

NOVELLO PUBLISHING LIMITED
14/15 Berners Street, London W1T 3LJ

It is requested that on all concert notices and programmes acknowledgement is made to 'The New Novello Choral Edition'.
Es wird gebeten, auf sämtlichen Konzertankündigungen und Programmen 'The New Novello Choral Edition' als Quelle zu erwähnen.
Il est exigé que toutes les notices et programmes de concerts, comportent des remerciements à 'The New Novello Choral Edition'.

Cover illustration: title page of the first edition of *Olivet to Calvary* (1904).

Published in Great Britain by Novello Publishing Limited
Head Office: 14/15 Berners Street, London W1T 3LJ, UK

Exclusive distributors:
Hal Leonard Europe Limited
Distribution Centre Newmarket Road,
Bury St Edmunds Suf f olk, IP33 3YB
www.halleonard.com

Printed in EU.

PREFACE TO THE FIRST EDITION

"Olivet to Calvary" recalls simply and reverently the scenes which mark the last few days of the Saviour's life on earth, and some of the reflections suggested thereby. The rejoicing of the multitude with hosannas and palms, the view of Jerusalem from the steep of Olivet, the lament over the beautiful city, the scene in the Temple, and the lonely walk back over the Mount at night, form the chief features of the first part.

Part II opens with the Supper of the Passover, at which Jesus washes His disciples' feet, and gives to his friends the new commandment of love for one another as the sign of true discipleship. From this the scene passes to the infinite pathos of the Garden of Gethsemane, the sudden appearance of the hostile crowd, Jesus forsaken by His disciples, His utter loneliness among ruthless foes, the tumult before Pilate in the Judgement Hall, the Passage of the Cross, the tragedy and triumph of Calvary.

REVISER'S NOTE

John Henry Maunder (1858-1920) was organist and choirmaster at a number of churches in South London. The first, and until now, only edition of *Olivet to Calvary* was published by Novello in 1904. There being no other source, revision has been confined to checking for internal inconsistencies and possible misprints. A few dynamics and articulation marks have been added editorially in square brackets, also a few additional suggestions for organ registration.

Michael Pilkington
Old Coulsdon, April 1998

NOTE

This revised edition of *Olivet to Calvary* follows the layout of the previous edition (catalogue number NOV070193) page for page, to allow this new edition to be used side-by-side with the edition it supersedes.

An arrangement of *Olivet to Calvary* for tenor and baritone soli, SATB and small orchestra (1.1.2.1./0.2.1.0./timp./org./stgs) by H.M. Higggs is available for hire from the publishers.

CONTENTS

PART I

PART II

OLIVET TO CALVARY

Words written and arranged by
Shapcott Wensley

J.H. MAUNDER

PART I

No. 1

On the way to Jerusalem

16
mf
His be-lov-ed Name. They made the path a - cross the mount, With
His be-lov-ed Name. They made the path With
leaf - y branch - es gay: And spread their robes with ea - ger hands, To
20
f
deck Mes - si - ah's way, And spread their robes with ea - ger hands, To deck Mes -
24
ff

29
-si - - ah's way.
-si - - ah's way.
-si - - ah's way.
-si - - ah's way.
29
f
Sw.
34
34
Gt.
Sw. mf
39
mf
His power has poured the light of Heaven, Up - on the sight-less eyes!
mf
His power has poured the light of Heaven, Up - on the sight-less eyes!
mf
His power has poured the light of Heaven, Up - on the sight-less eyes!
mf
His power has poured the light of Heaven, Up - on the sight-less eyes!
39
Unaccompanied ad lib.

44
His voice has thrilled the si - lent dead, And bade the sleep - er rise! Ho -
His voice has thrilled the si - lent dead, And bade the sleep - er rise! Ho -
His voice has thrilled the si - lent dead, And bade the sleep - er rise! Ho -
His voice has thrilled the si - lent dead, And bade the sleep - er rise! Ho -
f
48
- san - na to the Prince who comes, To free a race op - pressed! To drive the Gen - tile
- san - na! Ho - san - na to the Prince, Ho - san - na! Ho - san - na!
- san - na! Ho - san - na! Ho - san - na! Ho -
- san - na to the Prince who comes, To free a race op - pressed! To drive the Gen - tile
53
from our land, And make His peo - ple blest! To drive the Gen - tile from our land, And
Ho - san - na to the Prince who comes, To drive the Gen - tile from our land, And
- san - na! Ho - san - na to the Prince who comes, To drive the Gen - tile from our land, And
from our land, And make His peo - ple blest! To drive the Gen - tile from our land, And

58
make His peo - ple blest! Ho - san - na! Ho -
make His peo - ple blest! Ho - san - na! Ho -
make His peo - ple blest! Ho - san - na! Ho -
make His peo - ple blest! Ho - san - na! Ho -
ff
64
- sa - na! Bless - ed is the King of Is - rael!
- sa - na! Bless - ed is the King of Is - rael!
- sa - na! Bless - ed is the King of Is - rael!
- sa - na! Bless - ed is the King of Is - rael!
69
poco accel. to ♩ = 112
mf
Ho - san - na to the Son of Da - vid! Ho - san - na to the Son of
Ho - san - na to the Son of Da - vid! Ho - san - na to the Son of
Ho - san - na to the Son of Da - vid! Ho -
Ho - san - na to the Son of Da - vid! Ho -
mf

73
Da - vid! Bless - ed is He, bless - ed is He, bless - ed is He that
Da - vid! Bless - ed is He, bless - ed is He, bless - ed is He that
- san - na to the Son of Da - vid! Bless - ed is He, bless - ed is He that
- san - na to the Son of Da - vid! Bless - ed is He, bless - ed is He that
77
com - eth in the Name of the Lord! Ho - san - na in the
81
high - est! Ho - san - na in the high - est! Ho - san - na.

No. 2

Before Jerusalem

BARITONE [SOLO]
23
Recit.
p
And Je - sus paused, and gazed with tear - ful eyes, While the hushed mul - ti - tude stood
23
p
26
Andante (♩ = 88)
won - d'ring near.
26
Oboe Solo
pp
[senza Ped.]
32
Lamentoso
O Je -
32
p [Sw.]
[Ped.]
37
- ru - sa - lem! O Je - ru - sa - lem! Hadst thou but known
37
42
cresc.
cresc.
rall.
in this thy day, E - ven thou, e - ven thou, the things which be - long un - to
42
colla voce.

a tempo
peace, – But now they are hid from thine eyes!
Oboe Solo
mp
p
Oboe
sempre lamentoso
For the days shall come up - on thee, When thine
[Sw.]
en - e - mies shall com - pass thee a - round! They shall dash thee to the ground, Thee,
and thy chil - dren with - in thee! Hadst thou but known, O Je -
mp
rall. e dim.
- ru - sa - lem, hadst thou but known, hadst thou but known.
p
colla voce

No. 3

In the Temple

cresc.
Thine! Drive far a - way the sin that would en - snare; O cleanse Thy courts, and
bless Thine al - tar there. No voice but Thine can make it free, From
mp
accel. to ♩ = 96
molto agitato
all that is un - worth - y Thee! Temp - ta - tions' wiles Thy
f
mf
sa - cred courts as - sail! Temp - ta - tions' wiles Thy sa - cred courts as -
- sail! O hear my cry! O hear my cry!

O hear my cry! then shall my soul pre - vail!
mf Tempo 1mo
An - o - ther tem - ple waits Thee, Lord di - vine, The tem - ple of my heart, O make it Thine!
accel.
O make it Thine! O make it Thine! O hear my cry!
dim.
The tem - ple of my heart, O make it

77
Larghetto (♩ = 88)
thine.
CHORUS SOPRANO
ALTO
mp TENOR
Bow down Thine ear, O Lord,
mp BASS
Bow down Thine ear, O Lord,
mp
81
bow down Thine ear, O Lord, for I am poor, am
bow down Thine ear, O Lord, for I am poor, am
85
mp
Bow down Thine ear, O Lord,
mp
Bow down Thine ear, O Lord,
poor and in mis - - er - y, Bow down Thine ear, O Lord,
poor and in mis - - er - y, Bow down Thine

90
bow down Thine ear, O Lord, for I am poor, am poor and in
bow down Thine ear, O Lord, for I am poor, am poor and in
bow down Thine ear, O Lord, for I am poor and in
ear, O Lord, bow Thine ear, for I am poor, am poor and in
90
95
mis - - er - y. Look up-on mine ad -
mis - - er - y.
mis - - er - y. Look up-on mine ad - ver - si-ty
mis - - er - y. Look up-on mine ad - ver - si-ty
95
100
f
dim.
-ver - si-ty and mis - er - y, and mis - er - y, and for - give me all my
and mis - er - y, and mis - er - y, and for - give me all my
and mis - er - y, and mis - er - y, and for - give me all my
and mis - er - y, and mis - er - y, and for - give me all my
100

104
poco accel. (♩ = 112)
sin.
Turn Thee a-gain, O Lord, and let Thine an-ger cease from us,
sin.
sin.
sin.
104
poco accel. (♩ = 112)
109
turn Thee a-gain, O Lord, and let Thine an-ger cease from us, turn Thee a-gain, O
turn Thee a-gain, O Lord, and let Thine an-ger cease from us, turn Thee a-gain, O
turn Thee a-gain, O Lord, and let Thine an-ger cease from us,
turn Thee a-gain, O Lord, and let Thine an-ger cease from us,
109
[Gt.]
114
cresc.
f
Lord, turn Thee a-gain, O Lord, turn Thee a-gain, O
Lord, turn Thee a-gain, O Lord, turn, O
turn Thee a-gain, O Lord, turn Thee a-gain, O Lord,
turn Thee a-gain, O Lord, turn Thee a-gain, O Lord,
114
cresc.

118
Lord, and let Thine an - ger cease from us, and let Thine an - ger cease from
turn Thee a - gain and let Thine an - ger cease from us, and let Thine an - ger cease from
124
us, turn Thee a - gain, O Lord, turn Thee a - gain, O Lord. An -
[Sw.]
129
Tempo 1mo
- o - ther tem - ple waits Thee, Lord di - vine, The tem - ple of my heart, O make it

134
accel. agitato
Thine! Temp - ta - tions' wiles Thy sa - cred courts as - sail!
Thine! Temp - ta - tions' wiles Thy sa - cred courts as - sail!
Thine! Temp - ta - tions' wiles Thy sa - cred courts as - sail!
Thine! Temp - ta - - tions' wiles Thy sa - cred courts as - sail! temp -
134
accel. agitato
[Gt.]
139
cresc.
temp - ta - tions' wiles Thy sa - cred courts as - sail! O hear my
temp - ta - tions' wiles Thy sa - cred courts as - sail! O hear my
temp - ta - tions' wiles Thy sa - cred courts as - sail! O hear my
- ta - - - tions' wiles Thy sa - cred courts as - sail! O hear,
139
cresc.
144
cry! O hear my cry! O hear my cry!
cry! O hear my cry! O hear my cry!
cry! O hear my cry! O hear my cry!
O hear my cry! O hear my cry! O hear
144

149
Tempo 1mo
O hear, O hear my cry! An - o - ther tem - ple waits Thee, Lord di -
O hear, O hear my cry! An - o - ther tem - ple waits Thee, Lord di -
O hear, O hear my cry! An - o - ther tem - ple waits Thee, Lord di -
my cry! O hear my cry! An - o - ther tem - ple waits Thee, Lord di -
156
- vine, The tem - ple of my heart, O make it Thine!
- vine, The tem - ple of my heart, O make it Thine!
- vine, The tem - ple of my heart, of my heart, O make it Thine!
- vine, The tem - ple of my heart, O make it Thine! O
161
O make it Thine! O make it Thine! O hear my
O make it Thine! O make it Thine! O hear my
O make it Thine! O make it Thine! O hear my
make it Thine! O make it Thine! O hear my

166
cry!
The tem - ple of my heart, O
cry!
The tem - ple of my heart, O
cry!
The tem - ple of my heart, O
cry!
The tem - ple of my heart, O
166
p
172
dim.
make it Thine!
dim.
make it Thine!
dim.
make it Thine!
dim.
make it Thine!
172
[Sw.]
p

No. 4 The Mount of Olives

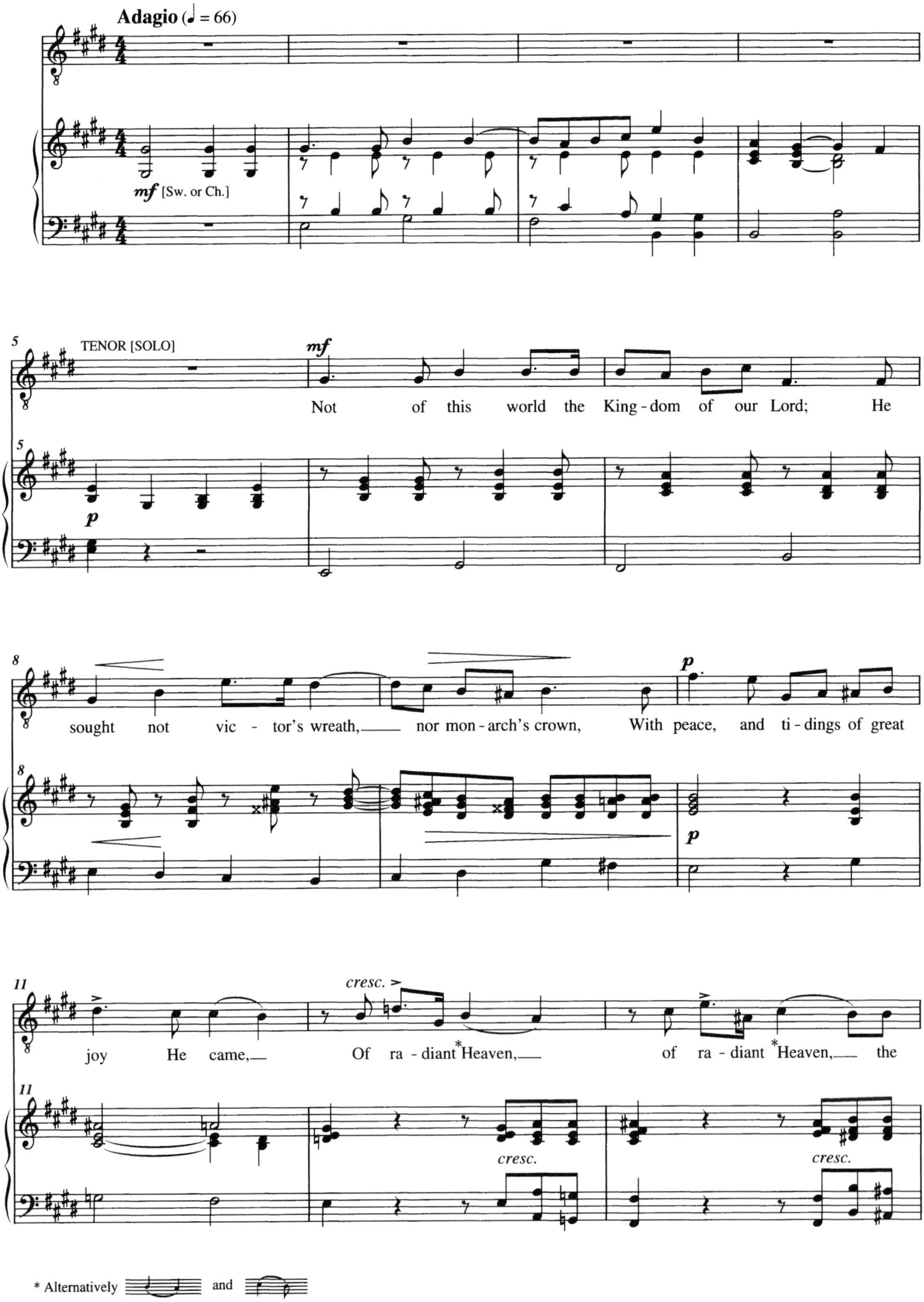

Adagio (♩ = 66)

mf [Sw. or Ch.]

5 TENOR [SOLO]

p

mf

Not of this world the King-dom of our Lord; He

8

sought not vic - tor's wreath, nor mon - arch's crown, With peace, and ti - dings of great

p

11

joy He came, Of ra - diant* Heaven, of ra - diant *Heaven, the

cresc.

* Alternatively 

14
Way, the Truth, the Life; A ho - ly guide through paths of night and
f
mf
17
time, He came to die that err - ing souls may live In sin - less
20
joy, where God's blest man - sions shine! He came to die that err - ing souls may
23
ff rit.
dim.
a tempo
cresc.
cresc.
live In sin - less joy, where God's blest man - sions shine! where God's blest
f
mf
26
f
rall.
man - sions shine!

29
Largo (♩. = 60)
[Sw.] mp
[senza Ped.]
34
CHORUS
SOPRANO
pp
'Twas night o'er lone - ly Ol - i -
ALTO
'Twas night o'er lone - ly Ol - i -
TENOR
'Twas night o'er lone - ly Ol - i -
BASS
'Twas night o'er lone - ly Ol - i -
[Ped.]
39
- vet, The trees their dark - some shad - ows
- vet, The trees their dark - some shad - ows
- vet, The trees their dark - some shad - ows
- vet, The trees their dark - some shad - ows

43
cast; And slow - - ly up the
cast; And slow - - ly up the
cast; And slow - - ly up the
cast; And slow - - ly up the
43
47
moun - - tain side, With wea - ry, wea - ry step the Sa - -
moun - - tain side, With wea - - ry, with wea - ry, wea - ry
moun - - tain side, With wea - ry, wea - ry
moun - - tain side, with wea - - ry, wea - ry, step the
47
51
cresc.
- - - viour passed. No joy - ous
cresc.
step the Sa - viour passed. No joy - ous
cresc.
step the Sa - viour passed. No joy - ous
cresc.
Sa - - viour passed. No joy - ous
51
cresc.

55
mul - ti - tude was there, No gar - ments
mul - ti - tude was there, No gar - ments
mul - ti - tude was there, No gar - ments
mul - ti - tude was there, No gar - ments
55
59
at His feet were thrown; The path that
at His feet were thrown; The path that
at His feet were thrown; The path that
at His feet were thrown; The path that
59
63
led to Beth - - a - - - ny, He trod in
led to Beth - - a - - - ny, He trod in
led to Beth - - a - - - ny, He
led to Beth - - a - - - ny, He trod in
63

67
sor - row and a - lone.
sor - - row and a - lone.
trod in sor - row and a - lone.
mp
The loud Ho -
sor - row and a - lone.
The loud Ho -
67
mp
72
dim.
-san - nas all were hushed,
The low - ly tri - umph
-san - nas all were hushed,
The low - ly tri - umph
72
dim.
79
dim.
of the day;
And fa - ding in the
of the day;
And fa - ding in the
79
dim.

85
moon - light pale, The branch - es strewn at morn - - ing lay.
moon - light pale, The branch - es strewn at morn - - ing lay.
92
mf
Thus o'er the brow of Ol - i - vet, The
Thus o'er the brow of Ol - i - vet, The
Thus o'er the brow of Ol - i - vet, The
Thus o'er the brow of Ol - i - vet, The
97
Sa - - - viour passed with wea - ry tread; The beasts have
Sa - - - viour passed with wea - ry tread; The beasts have
Sa - - - viour passed with wea - ry tread; The beasts have
Sa - - - viour passed with wea - ry tread; The beasts have
f
[Gt.]

101
lairs, the birds have nests, the beasts have
lairs, the birds have nests, the beasts have
lairs, the birds have nests, the beasts have
lairs, the birds have nests, the beasts have
101
105
lairs, the birds have nests, He had not
lairs, the birds have nests, He had not
lairs, the birds have nests, He had not
lairs, the birds have nests, He had not
105
109
where to lay His head! He had not
where to lay His head! He had not
where to lay His head! He had not
where to lay His head! He had not
109

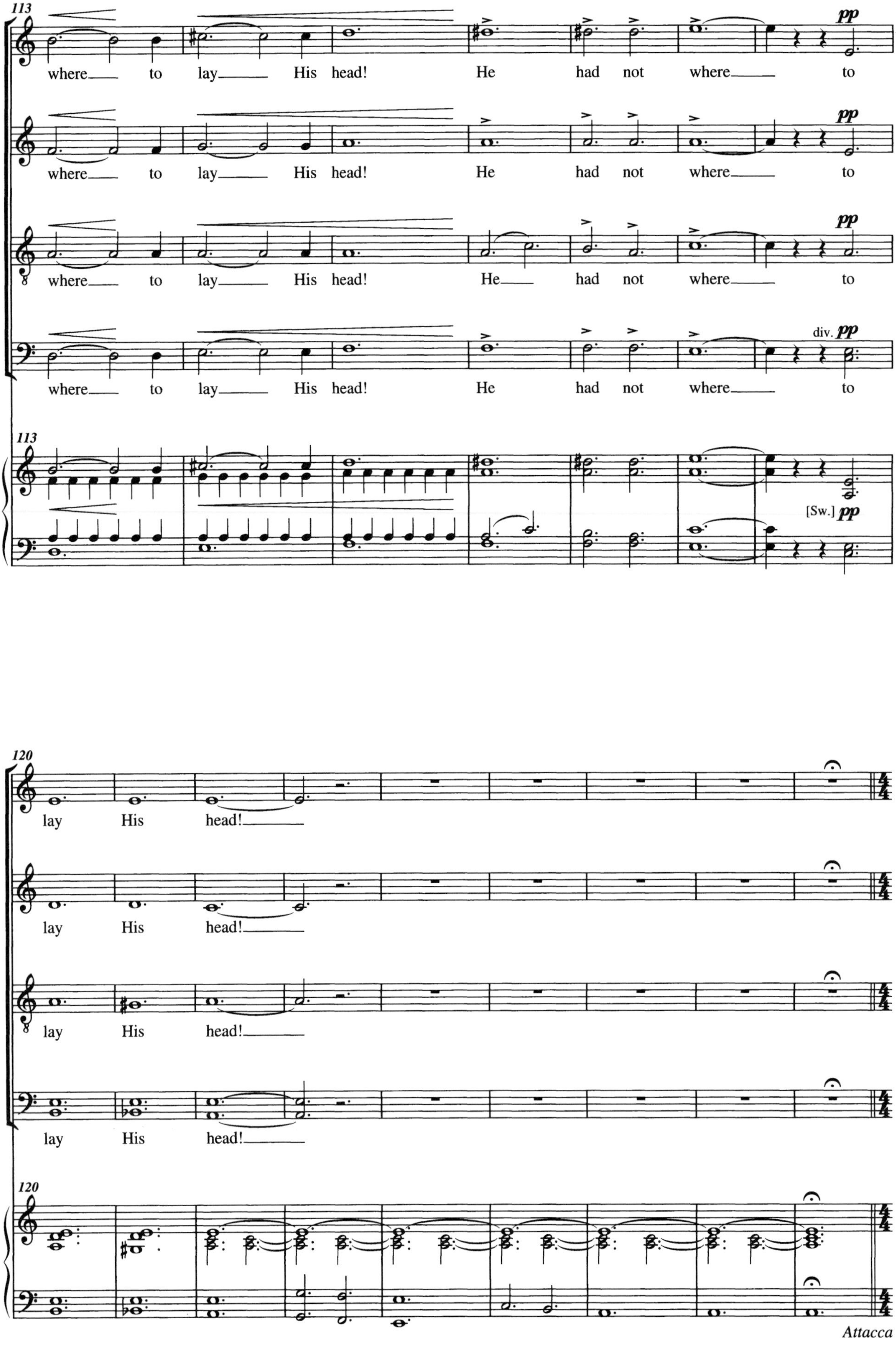

113

where to lay His head! He had not where to

pp

div.

[Sw.] *pp*

120

lay His head!

Attacca

Adagio (♩ = 60)
129
mp
TENOR [SOLO]
espressivo
He was des - pi - sed and re - jec - - ted of men, A
Adagio (♩ = 60)
Sw. pp
133
Man of sor - rows and ac - quaint - ed with grief, He was des - pi - sed,
136
He was re - jec - ted, A Man of sor - rows and ac - quaint - ed with grief,
139
A little faster (♩ = 66)
He was des - pi - sed, He was re - jec - ted. Not of
A little faster (♩ = 66)
mf

142
this world the King-dom of our Lord; He sought not vic-tor's wreath, nor mon-arch's crown; He came to
146
die that err-ing souls may live In sin-less joy, that err-ing souls may live where God's blest man-sions
f
ff
151
Grazioso (♩. = 56)
rall.
a tempo
shine.
BARITONE [SOLO]
mf espressivo
Come un-to Him, all ye that la-bour, and
mf
p
154
He will give you, will give you rest. Come un-to Him,
157
all ye that la-bour, and He will give you, will give you rest.
colla voce

160
CHORUS
p
Come un - to Him, all ye that la - bour, and He will give you, will
Come un - to Him, all ye that la - bour, and He will give you, will
Come un - to Him, all ye that la - bour, and He will give you, will
Come un - to Him, all ye that la - bour, and He will give you, will
160
Unaccompanied ad lib.
163
give you rest. Come un - to Him, all ye that la - bour, and
give you rest. Come un - to Him, all ye that la - bour, and
give you rest. Come un - to Him, all ye that la - bour, and
give you rest. Come un - to Him, all ye that la - bour, and
163
166
BARITONE [SOLO]
mf
Take His yoke up-on you, and
166
He will give you, will give you rest.
He will give you, will give you rest.
He will give you, will give you rest.
He will give you, will give you rest.
166

169
learn of Him, and
Take His yoke up-on you, and learn of Him
Take His yoke up-on you, and learn of Him
Take His yoke up-on you, and learn of Him
Take His yoke up-on you, and learn of Him
172
ye shall find rest un - to your souls. Come un - to Him, ye that are wea - ry,
176
Come, come, come!

Just as I am

Hymn for Congregation and Choir

Just as I am, though toss'd about
With many a conflict, many a doubt,
Fightings and fears within, without,
O Lamb of God, I come.

Just as I am, poor, wretched, blind;
cr. Sight, riches, healing of the mind,
Yea all I need, in Thee to find,
p O Lamb of God, I come.

Just as I am, (***mf***) Thou wilt receive,
Wilt welcome, pardon, cleanse, relieve;
cr. Because Thy promise I believe,
O Lamb of God, I come.

p Just as I am, (***mf***) (Thy love unknown
Has broken every barrier down),
cr. Now to be Thine, yea, Thine alone,
O Lamb of God, I come.

p Just as I am, (***mf***) of that free love
The breadth, length, depth, and height to prove,
cr. Here for a season, then above,
p O Lamb of God, I come.

Charlotte Elliott

END OF PART ONE

PART II

No. 5 A New Commandment

in - to a ba - son, and be - gan to wash His dis - ci - ples' feet.
ARIETTA
(♩ = 76)
cantabile
And He said, A new com - mand - ment give I un - to you, that ye
p Sw.
love one an - o - ther; e - ven as I have lov - ed you, so love ye one an -
cresc.
- o - ther. By this shall all men know
[Gt.]
cresc.
[senza Ped.]
that ye are Mine, by this shall all men know that ye are Mine,
[Ped.]

41
if ye have love one to an - o - ther, by this shall all men know that ye are Mine, by
45
rall.
a tempo
this shall all men know. A new com - mand - ment give I un - to you, That ye
p Sw.
49
poco accel.
love one an - o - ther, that ye love one an - o - ther; e'en as I have
54
Tempo 1mo
lov - ed you, e'en as I have lov - ed you, so love ye, so love ye,
cresc.
59
so love ye one an - o - ther.
colla voce.
dim.
p
pp

Quartet or Semi-Chorus

(Unaccompanied)

16
ff
though the Cross was near, A star 'mid deep'-ning shad - ows, E'en though the Cross was
though the Cross was near. A star 'mid deep'-ning shad - ows, E'en though the Cross was
though the Cross was near. A star 'mid deep'-ning shad - ows, E'en though the Cross was
though the Cross was near. A star 'mid deep'-ning shad - ows, E'en though the Cross was
16
21
p
pp
mf
near, e'en though the Cross was near. Thou ev - er blest Re - deem - er, En -
near, e'en though the Cross was near. Thou ev - er blest Re - deem - er, En -
near, e'en though the Cross was near. Thou ev - er blest Re - deem - er, En -
near, e'en though the Cross was near. Thou ev - er blest Re - deem - er, En -
21
27
- throned in Heav'n a - bove, O help Thy earth - ly pil - grims, To love as Thou dost love! Though
- throned in Heav'n a - bove, O help Thy earth - ly pil - grims, To love as Thou dost love! Though
- throned in Heav'n a - bove, O help Thy earth - ly pil - grims, To love as Thou dost love! Though
- throned in Heav'n a - bove, O help Thy earth - ly pil - grims, To love as Thou dost love! Though
27

33
dark and wild the path - way, Our feet shall nev - er tire, If to our souls Thou giv - est That
f
33
39
spark of sa - cred fire! If to our souls Thou giv - est That spark of sa - cred fire! that
ff
39
45
spark of sa - cred fire! that spark, that spark of sa - cred fire!
sf
sustain ff
45

No. 6 Gethsemane

Thy Will Be Done

Hymn for Congregation and Choir

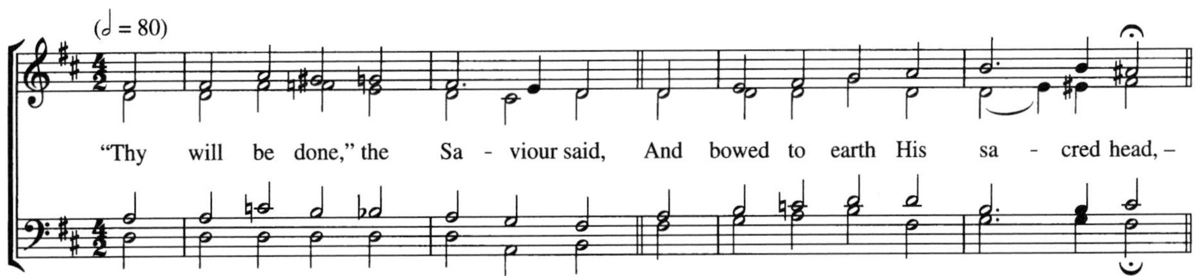

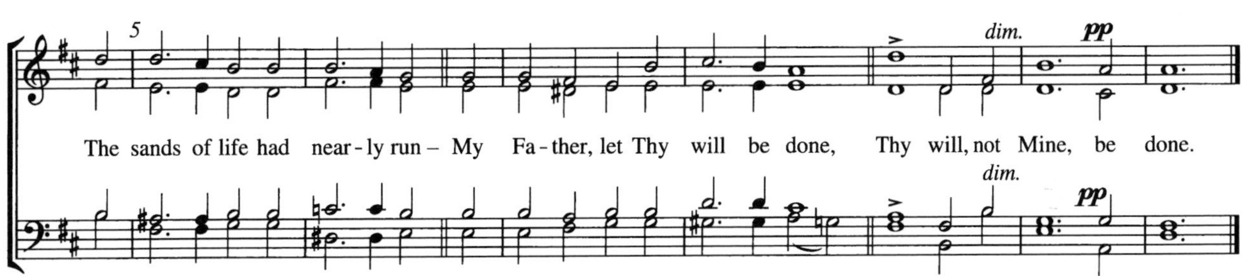

2 No watch His spent disciples kept,
Amid the shadows deep they slept;
But silent Angels waiting there,
Beheld His agony of prayer.
Thy will, not Mine, be done.

3 His soul foresaw the cruel scorns,
The brutal scourge, the crown of thorns,
And, darker than Gethsemane,
The shadows of the accursed tree.
Thy will, not Mine, be done.

4 What though He felt in that dread hour,
The storm of human passion lower!
Nor pain, nor death His soul would shun, –
My Father, let Thy will be done,
Thy will, not Mine, be done.

No. 7

Betrayed and Forsaken

A little slower (♩ = 88)
cresc.
torch - es.
And they took Je - sus, and bound Him, and led Him a -
-way.
Then all, all His dis - ci - - ples for -
- sook Him and fled.
Sw. p
cresc.

Andante (♩ = 76)
TENOR [SOLO]
O was there ev - er lone - li-ness like His!
Andante (♩ = 76)
Solo
[senza Ped.]
From the dear gar - den of His ag - o - ny The
Sw.
sin - less One was led.
His fol-lowers all for - sook their Lord and fled;
No gen - tle tone,
no kind-ly glance was there,
[Solo]
cresc.
[Ped.]

15
cresc.
cresc.
But mock - ing fa - ces, and harsh words of hate, The cru - el sol - diers,
cresc.
18
the un - pi - tying
the un - pitying crowd. Des - pised of men, re - jec - ted and for - sa - ken!
ff
21
rall.
Andante espressivo (♩ = 84)
O was there ev - er lone - li - ness like His!
colla voce
mp [Ch.]
26
mf molto espressivo
Ye who sin, and ye who sor - row,
Sw. p
31
Ye who in tempt - a - tion fall; See, O see your blest Re - deem - er,

Standing in the judgment hall. See Him beaten and derided,
See His flesh by scourges torn; Turn to Him, rememb'ring ever, 'Twas for
you, 'twas for you the stripes were borne.
Standing 'mid the
mocking soldiers, In the purple robe of scorn; See His gaze of gentle pity,
dim.
colla voce
f
p
mp [Ch.]
Sw. p

From beneath the pierc - ing thorn. Turn to Him ye hea-vy la - den,
Ye who toil, and ye who mourn; Lo! He looks in love up -
-on you, 'Twas for you, 'twas for you, the pain was
borne, 'twas for you, 'twas for you, 'twas for you the
pain was borne.
cresc.
dim.
f
ff
p
pp
ppp

No. 8

Before Pilate

* The part of Pilate may be sung by either a Baritone or a Tenor voice.

Allegro agitato (♩ = 116)
said, Be-hold your King!
And they cried out say - - ing,
ff [Gt.]
Cru - ci - fy Him! cru - ci - fy Him! cru - ci - fy Him!
cru - ci - fy Him! cru - - ci - fy Him!
He

He stir-reth up the peo-ple,
He stir-reth up the peo-ple,
stir-eth up the peo-ple, He stir-eth up the peo-ple Cru-
stir-eth up the peo-ple, He stir-eth up the peo-ple Cru-
Cru-ci-fy Him! cru-ci-fy Him!
Cru-ci-fy Him! cru-ci-fy Him!
-ci-fy Him! cru-ci-fy Him!
-ci-fy Him! cru-ci-fy Him!
cru-ci-fy Him! cru-ci-fy Him! cru-ci-fy Him!
cru-ci-fy Him! cru-ci-fy Him! cru-ci-fy Him!
cru-ci-fy Him! cru-ci-fy Him! cru-ci-fy Him!
cru-ci-fy Him! cru-ci-fy Him! cru-ci-fy Him!

36
PILATE
Shall I cru - ci - fy your King?
shall I cru - ci - fy your
f
39
King?
shall I cru - ci - fy your King?
f
We
f
We
[simile]
f
43
f
We have no king but Cæ - sar! we have no king but
f
We have no king but Cæ - sar! we have no king but
ff
have no king but Cæ - sar, we have no king but Cæ - sar! we have no king but
ff
have no king but Cæ - sar, we have no king but Cæ - sar! we have no king but
ff

46
Cæ - sar! A - way with this man,
Cæ - sar! A - way with this man,
Cæ - sar! A - way with this man, and re - lease un - to us Bar-
Cæ - sar! A - way with this man, and re - lease un - to us Bar-
[mf]
50
[mf cresc.]
and re - lease un - to us Bar - ab - bas, Bar - ab - bas, Bar - ab - bas, Bar-
and re - lease un - to us Bar - ab - bas, Bar - ab - bas, Bar - ab - bas, Bar-
-ab - bas, Bar - ab - bas, Bar - ab - bas, Bar-
-ab - bas, Bar - ab - bas, Bar - ab - bas, Bar-
[f]
cresc.
54
-ab - bas, A - way with this man, A - way with this man,
-ab - bas, A - way with this man, A - way with this man,
-ab - bas, A - way with this man, A - way with this man,
-ab - bas, A - way with this man, A - way with this man,

57
ff
Cru - ci - fy Him! cru - ci - fy Him! cru - - ci - fy Him!
Cru - ci - fy Him! cru - ci - fy Him! cru - - ci - fy Him!
Cru - ci - fy Him! cru - ci - fy Him! cru - - ci - fy Him!
Cru - ci - fy Him! cru - ci - fy Him! cru - - ci - fy Him!
Slower (♩ = 96)
61
PILATE
mf
Take ye Him, take ye Him and cru - ci - fy Him!
Sw. pp
67
for I find no fault in Him at all.
Lamentoso
(♩ = 100)
73
p Sw. Ob.
Ch. Lieb. Ged 8ft.
Sw.
Ch.
77
Sw.
Ch.
Sw.

No. 9 The March to Calvary

26
cresc.
30
Sw. p
34
CHORUS
SOPRANO
mf
The Sa - - viour
ALTO
mf
The Sa - - viour
TENOR
mf
The Sa - - viour
BASS
mf
The Sa - - viour
34
Gt. mf
38
King goes forth to die! Goes forth in
cresc.
King goes forth to die! Goes forth in
cresc.
King goes forth to die! Goes forth in
cresc.
King goes forth to die! Goes forth in
cresc.
38
cresc.

42
dim.
p
all His glo - ry bright! And An - gels
[Sw.] p
46
from the realms on high, Look down to
50
dim.
f
see the won - rous sight. On, on to
[Gt.] f

54
Cal - - vary's fate - - ful hill, Re - viled by
58
those He came to bless; But in His
p
p [Sw.]
62
suf - - f'ring bear - - - ing still The ma - - jes -
cresc.

66
dim.
p
-ty of Right - - eous - ness! The Sa - - viour
3
dim. 3
70
pp
King goes forth to die!
Sw. Reed. p
Ped. 16 ft.
76
sempre p

With wea - - ri - - ness and an - - guish
sore, On, on to death the Sa - - viour
goes! The Ro - - man hel - - mets flash be -
cresc.
ff
[Gt.]

94
-fore, Be - hind Him shout ex - ult - - ant foes. The
p
99
Son of God goes forth to die! To yield in
sempre p
104
pain His mor - - tal breath! To rob the
pp
ff
[Sw.]
[Gt.]

108
grave of Vic - - to - ry, And take, for aye the
grave of Vic - - to - ry, And take, for aye the
grave of Vic - - to - ry, And take, for aye the
grave of Vic - - to - ry, And take, for aye the
108
113
pp
sting from death! The Sa - - viour King goes forth to
sting from death! The Sa - - viour King goes forth to
sting from death! The Sa - - viour King goes forth to
sting from death! The Sa - - viour King goes forth to
113
pp [Sw.]
119
die!
die!
die!
die!
119
p

No. 10 Calvary

Recitative (Baritone) and Chorus: "Droop, Sacred Head"

[BARITONE SOLO]

(♩ = 100) *mf*

And when they came to the place which is call - ed Cal - va - ry,

(♩ = 100) Sw.8 ft. *p*

6 *p* there they cru - - ci - fied Him. And it was now a - bout the

11 sixth hour, and a dark - ness came o - ver the whole land un - til the ninth hour, the sun's light

colla voce. Sw. Voix Céleste and soft 16 ft.

15 fail - ing; and the veil of the tem - ple was

***f* accel.**

accel. Gt. *f*

19 rent in the midst. And when

Tempo I mo

reduce to Sw. *p*

[senza Ped.]

Adagio (♩ = 69)
espressivo
Je - sus had cried with a loud voice, He said, Fa - ther, in - to
Adagio (♩ = 69)
pp
Ped. soft 16 ft.
Thy hands I com - mend my spi - - - rit. And He bowed His
pp al fine
head and gave up the ghost.
Larghetto sostenuto (♩ = 92)
Larghetto sostenuto (♩ = 92)
Sw. p
cresc.
[senza Ped.]
SOPRANOS (or SOLO)
With great feeling
Droop, Sa - cred Head, Up - on that breast di -

48
cresc.
-vine, The strife is o'er The vic - to - ry is Thine.
53
p
Hush, sounds of earth, Sink, sink thou mourn - ful sun; On Cal - - vary's
cresc.
58
cross, Lo! Mer - cy's work is done, On Cal - - vary's cross, Lo! Mer - cy's
63
work is done.
[Ped.]

69
SOPRANO
ALTO
TENOR
BASS
p
cresc.
Droop, Sa - cred Head, Up - on that breast di - vine, The strife is
Droop, Sa - cred Head, Up - on that breast di - vine, The strife is
Droop, Sa - cred Head, Up - on that breast di - vine, The strife is
Droop, Sa - cred Head, Up - on that breast di - vine, The strife is
74
o'er, The vic - to - ry is Thine. Hush, sounds of earth, Sink,
o'er, The vic - to - ry is Thine. Hush, sounds of earth, Sink,
o'er, The vic - to - ry is Thine. Hush, sounds of earth, Sink,
o'er, The vic - to - ry is Thine. Hush, sounds of earth, Sink,
79
sink thou mourn - ful sun; On Cal - vary's cross, Lo! Mer - cy's work is done, On
sink thou mourn - ful sun; On Cal - vary's cross, Lo! Mer - cy's work is done, On
sink thou mourn - ful sun; On Cal - vary's cross, Lo! Mer - cy's work is done, On
sink thou mourn - ful sun; On Cal - vary's cross, Lo! Mer - cy's work is done, On

85
Cal - vary's cross, Lo! Mer-cy's work is done.
Cal - vary's cross, Lo! Mer-cy's work is done.
Cal - vary's cross, Lo! Mer-cy's work is done.
Cal - vary's cross, Lo! Mer-cy's work is done.
85
91
mf
Gaze, mor-tal, gaze, The Sa-viour hangs for thee,
mf
Gaze, mor-tal, gaze, The Sa-viour hangs for thee,
mf
Gaze, mor-tal, gaze, The Sa-viour hangs for
mf
Gaze, mor-tal, gaze, The Sa-viour hangs for
91
mp
97
dim.
poco cresc.
Si - lent in death, Up - on th'ac-curs-ed tree. Gaze, mor-tal, gaze, The
dim.
poco cresc.
Si - lent in death, Up - on th'ac-curs-ed tree. Gaze, gaze, mor-tal,
dim.
poco cresc.
thee, Si - lent in death, Up - on th'ac-curs-ed tree. Gaze, mor-tal,
dim.
poco cresc.
thee, Si - lent in death, Up - on th'ac-curs-ed tree. Gaze, mor-tal,
97
dim.

103
poco cresc.
Sa - viour hangs for thee, Si - lent in death, Up - on th'ac - curs - ed
gaze, The Sa - viour hangs for thee, Si - lent in death, Up -
gaze, The Sa - viour hangs for thee, Si - lent in death, Up -
gaze, The Sa - viour hangs for thee, Si - lent in death, Up -
108
molto cresc.
tree. Love, ho - liest love, Shall earth and heaven a - tone, In
- on th'ac - curs - ed tree. Love, ho - liest love, Shall earth and heaven a -
- on th'ac - curs - ed tree. Love, ho - liest love, Shall earth and heaven a -
- on th'ac - curs - ed tree. Love, ho - - - liest love, Shall
[Gt.]
113
fade - - less day, In fade - less day, From Christ's e -
- tone In fade - less day, In fade - less day, From Christ's e -
- tone In fade - less day, In fade - - less day, In Christ's e -
earth and heaven a - tone, In fade - - less day, From Christ's e -

118
div.
unis.
-ter - nal throne! In fade - less day, From Christ's e - ter - - - - nal
-ter - nal throne! In fade - less day, From Christ's e - ter - - - - nal
-ter - nal throne! In fade - less day, From Christ's e - ter - - - - nal
-ter - nal throne! In fade - less day, From Christ's e - ter - - - - nal
118
124
accel.
throne!
throne!
throne!
throne!
124
accel.

Rock of ages, cleft for me

Hymn for Congregation and Choir

2 Not the labours of my hands
Can fulfil Thy law's demands;
Could my zeal no respite know,
Could my tears for ever flow,
All for sin could not atone;
Thou must save, and Thou alone.

p 3 Nothing in my hand I bring,
Simply to Thy Cross I cling;
Naked, come to Thee for dress;
Helpless, come to Thee for grace;
Foul, I to the Fountain fly;
cresc. Wash me, Saviour, [*p*] or I die.

pp 4 While I draw this fleeting breath,
When my eyelids close in death,
cresc. When I soar through tracts unknown,
See Thee on Thy Judgment Throne;
p Rock of ages, cleft for me,
Let me hide myself in Thee. Amen.

Rev. A.M. Toplady

Published by Novello Publishing Limited
Music set by Stave Origination